ITALIANS IN AMERICA

web enhanced at www.inamericabooks.com

ALISON BEHNKE

LERNER PUBLICATIONS COMPANY / MINNEAPOLIS

Current information and statistics quickly become out of date. That's why we developed **www.inamericabooks.com**, a companion website to the **In America** series. The site offers lots of additional information—downloadable photos and maps and up-to-date facts through links to additional websites. Each link has been carefully selected by researchers at Lerner Publishing Group and is regularly reviewed and updated. However, Lerner Publishing Group is not responsible for the accuracy or suitability of material on websites that are not maintained directly by us. It is recommended that students using the Internet be supervised by a parent, a librarian, a teacher, or other adult.

Lerner Publications Company
A division of Lerner Publishing Group
241 First Avenue North
Minneapolis, MN 55401 U.S.A.

Website address: www.lernerbooks.com

Library of Congress Cataloging-in-Publication Data

Behnke, Alison.
    Italians in America / by Alison Behnke.
        p.   cm. — (In America)
    Summary: Examines the history of Italian immigration to the United States, discussing why they came, what they did when they got here, where they settled, and customs they brought with them.
    Includes bibliographical references and index.
    ISBN: 0-8225-4696-5 (lib. bdg. : alk. paper)
    1. Italian Americans—Juvenile literature. [1. Italian Americans.]
I. Title. II. In America (Minneapolis, Minn.)
E184.I8 B44 2005
973'.0451—dc21   2002015765

Manufactured in the United States of America
1 2 3 4 5 6 – BP – 10 09 08 07 06 05

CONTENTS

INTRODUCTION

In America, a walk down a city street can seem like a walk through many lands. Grocery stores sell international foods. Shops offer products from around the world. People strolling past may speak foreign languages. This unique blend of cultures is the result of America's history as a nation of immigrants.

Native peoples have lived in North America for centuries. The next settlers were the Vikings. In about A.D. 1000, they sailed from Scandinavia to lands that would become Canada, Greenland, and Iceland. In 1492 the Italian navigator Christopher Columbus landed in the Americas, and more European explorers arrived during the 1500s. In the 1600s, British settlers formed colonies that, after the Revolutionary War (1775–1783), would become the United States. And in the mid-1800s, a great wave of immigration brought millions of new arrivals to the young country.

Immigrants have many different reasons for leaving home. They may leave to escape poverty, war, or harsh governments. They may want better living conditions for themselves and their children. Throughout its history, America has been known as a nation that offers many opportunities. For this reason, many immigrants come to America.

Moving to a new country is not easy. It can mean making a long, difficult journey. It means leaving home and starting over in an unfamiliar place. But it also means using skill, talent, and determination to build a new life. The In America series tells the story of immigration to the United States and the search for fresh beginnings in a new country—in America.

ITALIANS IN AMERICA

Italians have been in America for a long time. Hundreds of years before the United States even became a nation, Italian explorers had landed on its shores. Colonists and other settlers arrived later. But large waves of Italian immigrants did not begin coming to the United States until about 1880. Throughout the late 1800s and early 1900s, thousands of Italians left their homeland behind. Faced with the extreme poverty and hardship of farm life in southern Italy, they headed for America.

Italian immigrants to America arrived by the thousands in the late 1800s. They struggled to find jobs, homes, and a place for themselves. The road was not always easy. They faced many challenges in their new country. But in time, Italian Americans became an important part of life in the United States. Like other immigrant groups, Italians have held on to many of their traditions, while also adopting new American customs. In the year 2000, the U.S. census showed that nearly sixteen million Americans of Italian ancestry were living in the United States. Italian Americans are neighbors, teachers, doctors, and businesspeople. They are athletes, students, entertainers, shopkeepers, and politicians. The wide-ranging contributions of Italians in America are difficult to measure. Throughout this country's history, Italian Americans have established themselves as leaders in many ways. And with imagination, determination, and spirit, they continue to enrich life and culture in the United States.

1

THE OLD COUNTRY

The nation of Italy is located in southern Europe, on a boot-shaped peninsula that stretches into the blue waters of the Mediterranean Sea. Italy also includes two large islands called Sicily and Sardinia, plus many other, smaller islands. Central and northern Italy are rugged and mountainous, with cool summers and snowy winters. The weather is milder along Italy's coasts, where it is usually sunny and warm. The nation's capital is Rome, a large city in central Italy.

AN ANCIENT LAND

Italy is often called the old country, and it is indeed old. Its history stretches back for thousands of years, to a time long before the region even became the nation of Italy. Historians think that the first Italians came to the area about two hundred thousand years ago. Around the 900s or 800s B.C., people

Etruscan frescoes— paintings done on wet plaster—such as the one above give historians clues about the lives of early Italians. In this fresco from an Etruscan tomb, the man is thought to be a priest or a mourner for the deceased.

called the Etruscans settled the Italian Peninsula. The Etruscans were good sailors and traders. Their cities grew to be rich and powerful.

One of the cities under Etruscan control was Rome. At that time, Rome was a large farming community. The Romans eventually developed their own type of government. They were not willing to be ruled by Etruscan kings any longer. In 510 B.C., they overthrew the king and founded the Roman Republic. The republic was a state without a king or queen. Instead, a group of leaders formed the Senate to run the republic. The Roman Republic had strong, well-trained armies. They overpowered the Etruscans and other settlers, and Rome eventually took control of the entire Italian Peninsula.

Rome's leaders were soon hungry for more land, and its armies went on to conquer areas in Europe and Africa. But growing power also brought trouble to the republic. While wealthy Romans got richer and richer, laborers lived hard lives of poverty and toil. Revolts broke out. At the same time, Rome's military and political leaders began to fight each other for control. Civil war erupted in the republic.

7

Roman emperors including Trajan (far right, holding scroll) *led military campaigns to win the empire land, wealth, and power.*

After the wars, a new system emerged. In 27 B.C., the emperor Augustus took power, and the Roman Republic became the Roman Empire. Instead of having a democratic system with many leaders, the empire had one all-powerful ruler. For many years, the empire continued to grow. It became a great civilization that produced artists, poets, and philosophers. But eventually it was too large and spread out to be stable. Rome's leaders could not protect it from the many outsiders who wanted a share in its power. By the end of the A.D. 400s, the empire on the Italian Peninsula had fallen apart.

ROME NOWADAYS IS ALL ABLAZE WITH GOLD, RICH WITH THE WEALTH OF THE WORLD THAT SHE HATH CONQUERED.

—*Ovid, an ancient Roman poet, writing in about A.D. 2*

8

Becoming a Nation

For hundreds of years after the fall of the Roman Empire, many different groups controlled the area. Invaders from northern Africa and from many parts of Europe ruled different parts of the peninsula. People formed communities called city-states. Sometimes the city-states cooperated or traded with each other, but they did not report to any national government. Each city-state had its own government and culture. Most even had their own dialects, or variations of the Italian language. The Italian Peninsula's many mountains and valleys separated these communities and made it difficult for people in different areas to communicate with each other. As regions developed their own unique customs, most people came to feel very loyal to their local communities.

A period called the Italian Renaissance began in the 1300s. Many Italian artists, writers, and philosophers wanted to make their culture as great as ancient Rome had been. Their ideas spread to other parts of Europe, and the Renaissance lasted into the 1600s.

The Renaissance painting (above) *by Masolino da Panicale, shows the Italian city of Florence. Florence was an important center of Renaissance art and culture.*

9

The years of the Renaissance resulted in important books, beautiful paintings, and impressive buildings. But life was still very hard for most people. The inhabitants of the Italian Peninsula faced poverty, war, and disease. Some of their rulers were harsh. They did not try to improve the lives of their subjects. In addition, political unrest troubled the region. At the beginning of the 1800s, Italy was still not one nation. It was divided into many small regions. Rulers from France, Spain, and other countries controlled most of these areas. Beginning in the 1820s, some Italians fought against the outside powers. They wanted to unify the country under an Italian leader. But the fight was unsuccessful. Many people were frustrated and unhappy.

Finally, in 1861 Italy became a united nation. A military hero named Giuseppe Garibaldi led troops to southern Italy and Sicily, capturing the regions from their foreign rulers. An Italian king was chosen to reign over all of Italy.

DAILY LIFE

Many Italians hoped that unification would improve conditions in Italy. Times were hard during the mid–1800s and into the beginning of the 1900s. A few people were rich and powerful, but most were poor. Some people thought that a national government would make sure that all parts of Italy got the money they needed. The poor farming regions of the south badly needed this help. But southerners were disappointed by the results of unification.

TO FIND MORE INFORMATION ON ITALIAN HISTORY, CULTURE, AND PEOPLE, VISIT WWW.INAMERICABOOKS.COM.

10

AN INTERNATIONAL HERO

Giuseppe Garibaldi *(right)* became a national hero in Italy after driving out the country's foreign rulers. But he was not just famous at home. Garibaldi was also something of a celebrity in the United States. The first Italian American newspaper, *L'Eco d'Italia*, helped Italians in America keep up with events in their homeland—including Garibaldi's adventures.

During the U.S. Civil War (1861–1865), President Abraham Lincoln even asked Garibaldi to command troops for the Union. Garibaldi did not take part in the Civil War, but other Italians did. More than two hundred Italians fought in the conflict, and the Italian American officer L. W. Tinelli organized a special group of foreign-born soldiers. He named it the Garibaldi Guard. In 1888 a statue of Garibaldi was presented by Italian Americans to the people of New York City, and the monument still stands in Washington Square.

Working the land with only basic tools, Italian farmers struggled to make a living.

Most of the country's money and development went to factories and farms in the northern part of the country.

Until the early 1900s, more than half of all Italians were farmers. But most of the tools and methods used on the country's farms were old fashioned and inefficient. In addition, most farmers didn't have enough money to buy their own land. They worked for landlords who paid them very little for their hard work. Even the farmers who did own small plots of land could barely grow enough food to feed themselves and their families.

In southern Italy, poor soil and bad weather made farming especially difficult. Crops struggled to grow in

12

the dry, rocky soil. Long, hot summers threatened the few crops that could be planted and harvested, such as wheat, grapes, oranges, and lemons. Rainfall was low, and the south's few rivers often ran dry. Water was scarce. The sun blazed down on dusty fields and hot, tired workers. And the crops that managed to survive the weather also had to face insects and other pests.

Southern Italy also faced natural disasters that threatened to ruin crops. Droughts—periods when the

This map shows Italy as it is in modern times. Most Italian emigrants in the late 1800s came from south of Naples. Download this and other maps at www.inamericabooks.com.

land did not get enough rain—were common. At other times, erupting volcanoes sent rivers of fiery lava streaming down mountainsides, burying fields and towns. Landslides and earthquakes were other dangers. In 1908 an earthquake hit southern Italy, followed by a huge, destructive tidal wave. The disaster flattened homes and killed thousands of people.

Farmers tried to make their land more productive. In the 1800s, they cut down trees to make more room for crops. But without trees to hold the dirt in place, rains washed away valuable soil. Floods followed, and the wet, marshy areas left by the floods were perfect breeding grounds for mosquitoes. The mosquitoes carried a deadly disease called malaria, and terrible outbreaks of the illness spread through southern Italy. Thousands of people sickened and died.

Life was different in northern Italy, but not much easier. Many people in the north worked in factories. These laborers usually made a little more money than farmers did. But wages were still low, and the work was hard. Many factories were not heated. They were freezing in the winter and terribly hot in the summer. Machinery sometimes malfunctioned and injured workers. Strict bosses made their employees work long hours with few breaks.

Some Italians fought for better jobs. They organized strikes during which laborers refused to work, and they planned protests demanding higher pay and safer working conditions. But the police usually put a stop to these activities.

TO READ THE WORDS OF OTHER IMMIGRANTS TO AMERICA, VISIT WWW.INAMERICABOOKS.COM.

DROUGHTS ARE THE TERROR OF OUR VALLEY AND OFTEN HAVE I SEEN PEOPLE WITH HUNGER IN THEIR EYES GAZING UPWARDS AT THE SERENE BLUE SKY AND BEGGING FOR RAIN.

—*Pascal D'Angelo, who immigrated to the United States in 1910, at the age of sixteen*

Having faced poverty, drought, and other challenges, this Sicilian family piles its belongings onto a cart and prepares to leave home.

The little money that most farmers and workers made did not go very far. Italians had to pay high taxes to the government. Many men also had to join the army. Their time in the army took them away from home and made it even harder for them to take care of their families.

Life was tough at home as well as on the job. Most farmers lived in villages and walked or rode donkeys for miles to and from the fields. A typical farmer's home of the time was only one room with a dirt floor, sometimes with a small loft up above. The main piece of furniture was usually a bed. Often, the whole family slept in this bed. Sometimes, especially during bad weather, people shared the main room with their livestock and other animals. Dirt or cobblestone streets ran between homes, which were constructed anywhere and out of anything that people could find. Some were straw huts. Others were

15

made in caves or in the ruins of ancient buildings. They did not have plumbing. Children often helped carry water for washing and cooking from streams and wells. After dark, fires and oil–burning lamps gave the only light. Large families, including children, parents, and grandparents, often lived together in tiny, cramped spaces.

But families did not spend very much time in the house. Southerners, especially, were outside most of the day, farming, tending animals, or doing other chores. Shoppers could stop at bakeries and produce stores to pick up food for the day's meals. In farmers' and workers' homes, these meals were usually simple. In the north, many people dined on a cornmeal dish called polenta. In both the north and the south, lentils, beans, bread, and soup were common foods.

When they weren't helping in the fields, Italian women in the late 1800s worked in the home. They were responsible for cooking, sewing, and child care.

LEARN MORE ABOUT LIFE IN ITALY AT WWW.INAMERICABOOKS.COM.

16

Families also enjoyed fresh fruits and vegetables. Pasta, meat, and sweets were special treats.

When they weren't working, many Italians went to their village's main square, called a piazza. Every Italian village, no matter how small, had a piazza. This central meeting place usually contained the local Roman Catholic church. Nearly all Italians followed Roman Catholicism, a branch of Christianity centered in Rome. The piazza was also a good place for people to gather and visit or take an evening stroll. Or they might choose to chat over a cup of coffee at a nearby café or over a glass of wine at a restaurant.

Italian families also had other ways to relax. When they had time, they played card games and bocce, a traditional Italian ball game. They enjoyed paying visits to friends and telling stories and singing songs. They celebrated religious holidays, festivals, and other special occasions.

Even during hard times, many Italian families enjoyed taking an evening stroll—called the passeggiata—*through their local piazzas.*

17

But none of these pastimes could change the harsh reality of poverty and hunger. Longing to escape, Italians began to look for a way out. To many people, it seemed as if the only way to survive was to leave their homes behind. A trickle of emigration (moving to other countries) had begun in the 1820s, as Italians left to escape the political troubles in their homeland. By the end of the century, that trickle had become a flood.

LEAVING HOME

Until the end of the 1800s, the Italian government did not want its citizens to emigrate. Leaders were worried that emigration would take away talented people that Italy needed at home. But Italy's population grew quickly between 1871 and 1905. There was not enough farmland for everyone who wanted it. The Italian government decided that emigration might be a good way to make the country less crowded.

At this time, the United States was going through an important change called the Industrial Revolution. People had discovered new sources of energy, such as natural gas and electricity. They built hundreds of new factories, filled with powerful machines. These growing factories needed more and more workers. American companies sent agents to Italy and other European countries to find workers. These agents promised good jobs to anyone who would come to the United States. And it was easier than it had ever been to go to the United States. New steamships made traveling across the Atlantic Ocean faster than it had been in the past. In addition, so many ships were making the journey between Europe and North America that tickets for these ships became quite inexpensive.

Not all Italians wanted to leave their homeland. New factories were springing up in the northern part of Italy, just as they were in the United States. Few northerners emigrated to America. They found jobs in Italian factories instead. But thousands of people in southern Italy lived in poverty. They loved their homes. But they were also

18

eager for a new beginning, and they saw promise in the United States.

To L'America

Sometimes whole families journeyed to L'America, as Italians called the United States. But in most cases, only one family member made the trip. Many men left their wives and children behind. Most farmers planned to work hard in America, save their money, and then return to buy farmland in their villages in Italy.

Publications like this one, showing Italian immigrants arriving joyfully in America, beckoned to poor farmers in southern Italy.

UP RUMBLED THE TRAIN WHICH TRAVELED WITHOUT ANY HORSES OR MULES. I FELT MY FATHER URGING ME ABOARD. A LAST KISS FROM MY MOTHER. EVERYTHING WAS OBSCURED BY A MIST OF TEARS. WE WERE GOING INTO THE UNKNOWN.

—*Pascal D'Angelo*

19

PART OF AMERICAN HISTORY

Large numbers of Italians first came to America in the late 1800s. But Italians have influenced American history since its earliest days. During the Middle Ages (A.D. 476–1450), European sailors traveled to Asia searching for gems, gold, and spices. To make these journeys, they had to sail all the way around Africa. The Italian navigator Christopher Columbus believed that there was a shorter route. In 1492 he sailed west in search of this route. Instead, he reached the coasts and islands of North, Central, and South America. To Europeans, this land was a new world. A few years after Columbus's first voyage, another Italian, Amerigo Vespucci, also traveled across the Atlantic Ocean. He published the story of his journey when he got home. Mapmakers began using Amerigo's name to refer to the new lands in the west. Eventually the two continents of the New World became know as the Americas.

Other early Italians in America were sent by the Roman Catholic Church. These travelers, called

Italian explorer Christopher Columbus lands in the New World.

20

The Italian navigator Amerigo Vespucci gave his name to America.

missionaries, tried to convert Native Americans to Christianity. Father Marcos de Niza was a missionary in Peru and Mexico in 1531. The Italian priest Eusebio Kino opened churches in northwestern Mexico and Arizona. Kino also explored and mapped the Colorado River and traveled to California.

Some Italians came to America as colonists. Italian musicians, artists, traders, and teachers arrived in colonies that had been established by English settlers. Filippo Mazzei came to America in the 1770s and settled in Virginia, where he became friends with future president Thomas Jefferson. In 1776 Italian Americans Caesar Rodney of Delaware and William Paca of Maryland signed the Declaration of Independence, proclaiming the colonies' freedom from England. Rodney rode his horse eighty miles through a rainstorm to sign the document, even though he was very sick. In honor of Rodney's dedication to American independence, his historic ride is shown on Delaware's state quarter.

Filippo Mazzei settled in colonial Virginia, becoming one of the first Italian Americans.

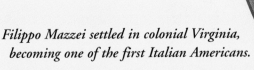

21

The ships that brought Italians and other immigrants across the Atlantic were crowded and uncomfortable. But they were also filled with the hopes and dreams of families looking for better lives in America.

People—some of whom had never left their native villages before—boarded noisy, smoky trains bound for Italy's large ports. Parents, children, husbands, and wives wept as they said good-bye. They had no way of knowing for sure if they would ever see each other again.

Deciding to leave for America could be hard. The journey itself

MANY PEOPLE ARE INTERESTED IN LEARNING ABOUT THEIR FAMILY'S HISTORY. THIS STUDY IS CALLED GENEALOGY. IF YOU'D LIKE TO LEARN ABOUT YOUR OWN GENEALOGY AND HOW YOUR ANCESTORS CAME TO AMERICA, VISIT WWW.INAMERICABOOKS.COM FOR TIPS AND LINKS TO HELP YOU GET STARTED.

AHEAD LAY THE STRANO PAESE [STRANGE LAND], AMERICA, THE STRANGE LAND WHERE IT WAS SAID THERE WAS WORK AND BREAD.

—Richard Gambino, an Italian American author and historian

was sometimes harder. Even on fast new ships, the voyage from Italy to the United States took two or three weeks. Emigrants could take only a few of their most treasured belongings. Most Italians could only afford tickets in the steerage section, which was located on the ship's lower decks. Hundreds of passengers were crammed together in crowded rooms. There was rarely enough space for everyone to lie down to sleep or to sit down to eat. There were no windows, and the air became heavy and stale. Illnesses spread quickly through the cramped quarters. Passengers could only go to the ship's upper decks when the weather was nice, and even then they took turns. Many travelers got seasick. But even in these uncomfortable conditions, Italian emigrants entertained themselves with music, singing, dancing, and card games. They shared stories of the villages that they had left behind, and they looked ahead with optimism. They were on their way to a new land, with new possibilities.

23

2

L'America

After making the long, difficult voyage to America, Italian immigrants were often tired and sick. Many of them were nervous about what awaited them in an unfamiliar place. But they were also eager to begin building new lives for themselves and to make the best of the opportunities they found.

ENTRY AT ELLIS ISLAND

Many early Italian immigrants stood on American soil for the first time at Castle Garden. Located on the southwestern tip of Manhattan in New York City, Castle Garden opened as a landing point for immigrants in 1855. But most Italians arrived after 1892, when the first stop for nearly all immigrants was Ellis Island. The Ellis Island Immigration Station sat on a small island in New York City's harbor. The station's job was to handle the large numbers of immigrants coming to the United States in the late 1800s. First- and second-class passengers could have their immigration papers processed on the ship. But the majority of immigrants, who rode in steerage, went to Ellis Island.

The great oceangoing ships that brought European immigrants across the Atlantic did not go all the way to the immigration station. Passengers transferred to smaller ferryboats that glided past the Statue of Liberty and docked at Ellis Island. Carrying battered suitcases and bundles, new arrivals made their way toward the station's main building.

The station's halls and rooms swarmed with people speaking many different languages. Immigrants often waited for a long time before getting any closer to America. First, a doctor examined each newcomer. Immigrants who were sick often had to stay at the

Ellis Island officials check newly arrived immigrants for trachoma, a highly contagious eye disease.

25

station until they were well. If they were seriously ill, they might be sent back to Italy. Next, immigrants answered a long series of questions. They said where they came from and whether they had any relatives in America. They also told the inspectors at the station how much money they had with them, whether they could read and write

> *Our compensation, besides our salaries, for the heartbreaking scenes we witnessed, was the realization that a large percentage of these people pouring into Ellis Island would probably make good and enjoy a better life than they had been accustomed to where they came from.*
>
> —*Fiorello La Guardia, who worked on Ellis Island before becoming mayor of New York City*

in any language, and whether they already had jobs waiting for them.

The examinations and the questions could be frightening. Most Italians did not speak English. They talked to the doctors and the inspectors through translators. They did not know if they would be allowed into the country or not. Some people were turned away. Others had to wait for days in uncomfortable conditions before being approved. To those Italians, Ellis Island was L'Isola delle Lacrime—"the Island of Tears." But to the new arrivals who were able to enter America, the future looked full of hope. They left Ellis Island with dreams of what lay ahead.

SETTLING IN THE STRANO PAESE

Some Italians who landed in the big cities of the *strano paese*—strange land—already knew people in America. When these newcomers arrived, they were greeted happily by *paesani*—people who came from the same villages back in Italy. Paesani helped each other find

Carrying the few belongings that they were able to bring from the old country, immigrants leave Ellis Island to begin exploring their new home.

TO DISCOVER SOME OF THE MANY STORIES FROM ELLIS ISLAND, VISIT WWW.INAMERICABOOKS.COM.

homes and jobs. They made this new country seem friendlier and safer.

Other immigrants were all alone. Overwhelmed by the unfamiliar surroundings, some of them were tricked by con artists who stole from them. Many of them sought out other Italians. Agents called *padroni*, most of whom were Italians who had already been in the country for a while, often offered to help newcomers find places to live and work. The padroni could be helpful, but many of them took advantage of bewildered new arrivals. Some charged very high fees for their services, forcing immigrants to hand over more than half of their income. Other padroni talked Italian workers into signing contracts that required them to work for a certain amount of time,

Agents called padroni (above) *could be helpful to a new Italian immigrant in a big city. But some padroni cheated workers out of their wages.*

usually under poor conditions and for low wages.

But even the immigrants who arrived by themselves rarely stayed alone for long. Italians clustered in cities where factories needed workers. They formed large populations in cities on the East Coast. America's first large Italian American community formed in New York City. Almost all Italian immigrants arrived in New York, and many of them settled there.

Gradually, Italian immigrants began to move beyond New York. Some settled in other eastern states, including Delaware, Pennsylvania, and Massachusetts. Some headed south to Maryland and Louisiana. And still others went west. They went looking for work, farmland, or an escape from the crowded cities of the east. Many of them worked in the mining towns of Colorado, Utah, and Wyoming. They boarded trains heading westward across the vast American continent. The nation of Italy is roughly the size of the state of Arizona. Gazing out the windows of the train during the long journey across America, Italians were amazed by the size of their new land.

As more immigrants made their way to the Pacific Coast from their starting point at Ellis Island, the city of San Francisco, California, developed an Italian community.

Most of the first arrivals were from northern Italy. Gold had been discovered in California's hills in 1849, and the stories of miners striking it rich drew some early Italian immigrants to San Francisco. Later, as immigration from Italy to America skyrocketed, hopeful southern Italians came seeking whatever opportunities they could find. San Francisco's Italian population grew quickly.

Italian immigrants also moved on to other cities from New York, and Italian neighborhoods formed all over the country. On the East Coast, a large Italian population settled in Boston, Massachusetts, in an area known as the North End. In Philadelphia, Pennsylvania, Italians lived in South Philly. Farther south, they made their homes near the port of Baltimore, Maryland. As more immigrants journeyed

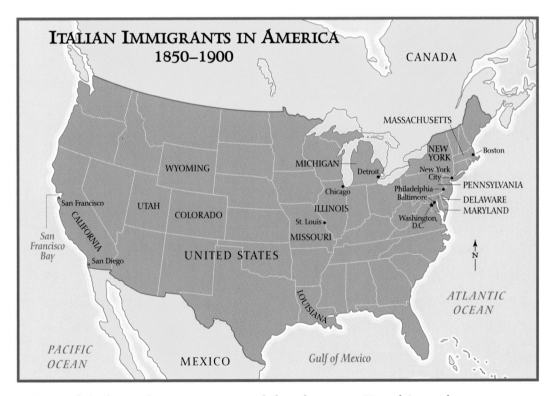

Many of the first Italian immigrants settled in the eastern United States, but some traveled farther west. Visit www.inamericabooks.com to download this map.

westward, communities also sprang up in Detroit, Michigan; Chicago, Illinois; St. Louis, Missouri; and San Diego, California.

THE OLD COUNTRY IN THE NEW WORLD

In New York and many other big cities, Italians lived in apartment houses called tenements. These buildings were often located in run-down parts of cities where earlier immigrant groups had once lived. Tenement landlords charged low rent that many immigrants could afford. But the apartments were

IN THIS COUNTRY IMMIGRANTS OF THE SAME TOWN STICK TOGETHER LIKE A SWARM OF BEES FROM THE SAME HIVE.

—*Pascal D'Angelo*

Many immigrant families lived in ramshackle tenements like this one. Although the housing was not luxurious, Italians took comfort in having paesani as their neighbors.

30

usually in bad shape. Most were unheated, and many of them did not have indoor bathrooms. The buildings were sometimes crumbling, and they were always cramped. A family of five or six people often crowded into one tiny room. Illnesses spread easily in these conditions. Diseases such as tuberculosis often swept through Italian immigrant communities with little warning.

In these dark, damp apartments, on the crowded streets, and amid the towering buildings of large American cities, many Italians yearned for their homeland. They missed the sunlight, open skies, and vast fields of Italy. Grouping together in close-knit communities, they tried to keep a bit of the old country alive in this new world. As more and more Italian immigrants arrived and settled throughout the country, "Little Italys" sprang up in cities with large Italian American populations.

In New York, the neighborhood around Mulberry Street came to be called Little Italy. In San Francisco,

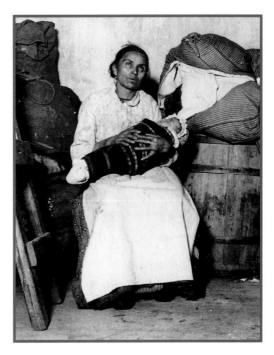

An Italian immigrant woman and her child make their home in a tiny apartment.

an Italian community formed in an area known as Telegraph Hill. As more newcomers arrived, the area expanded to include North Beach and Fisherman's Wharf. And, even in America, northern and southern Italians tended to live in separate areas. Immigrants from the same villages or districts in Italy lived in the same parts of Little Italys.

Italian-owned restaurants, bakeries, and cafés soon sprang up in these neighborhoods. Italian grocers set up shop selling pasta,

31

salami, bread, cheese, and coffee to immigrants hungry for a taste of home. Old-timers say that New York's first pizzeria opened on Spring Street, near Mulberry Street, in 1905. Other local businesses included drugstores, butcher shops, and barber shops. At one point, about 85 percent of New York City's barbers were of Italian descent.

After work, residents enjoyed spending time together. In San Francisco, a park called Washington Square took the place of the local piazzas where villagers had gathered in Italy. Neighbors in America also enjoyed sitting on their front steps to visit and enjoy the cool evening air. Some of their other pastimes were old favorites from Italy. Adults played bocce ball and cards. Children played games of stickball in New York's streets. People listened to music or made their own. Families gathered to share meals and to chat about their days.

Some Italian Americans joined neighborhood organizations that offered English lessons or that

In the heart of the nearest city one can find [regional Italian groups including] a Sicilian, a Calabrian, a Neapolitan, an Abruzzian village, all within a few blocks, and each with its peculiar traditions, manner of living, and dialect. In New York there are as many Italians as in the city of Rome; there are more Italians in Philadelphia than in Florence.

—*Enrico C. Sartorio, from his book* Social and Religious Life of Italians in America

sponsored clubs for boys and girls. Other community activities celebrated arts and culture from home, including operas, plays, and dance performances. Live theater and puppet shows were popular forms of entertainment for adults and children alike.

Fruit and vegetable vendors offer their goods to passing shoppers in a bustling street in New York's Little Italy. Newly arrived immigrants, who often knew little or no English, found it easiest to do business with other Italians.

"WE POOR LABORERS"

Close-knit neighborhoods offered Italian Americans familiar community and culture. But even tenements cost rent, and immigrants quickly set about finding work. After all, better opportunities were what they had come looking for in America. However, few Italians were able to work in the same kinds of jobs in America that they had had in Italy. Most of them did not speak English when they first came to the United States. This language barrier limited the kinds of jobs that they could get. And, although most immigrants had been farmers at home, affordable land was hard to come by.

Eager to work, Italian laborers accepted low wages. Most of them earned far less than did the average American, and, in some cases, less than members of other immigrant groups. Great numbers of

33

Italian American laborers take a break from building the New York City subway system.

newcomers found jobs in factories. Desperate to begin earning any money that they could, they were also willing to do some of the hardest, dirtiest, most unpleasant, and most dangerous jobs. Italians worked collecting garbage and cleaning sewers. Some of them became "rag pickers"—people who dug through waste to find bits of cloth or metal that they could sell.

Many Italian Americans on the East Coast found construction jobs. In New York, as the city grew, Italians helped build the skyscrapers that towered above the streets. They worked at digging the subways that ran below the streets. Throughout the country, Italians helped construct streets and railroads. The foremen who watched over construction crews often

YOUR RAILROADS, YOUR PUBLIC BUILDINGS, YOUR COAL ARE WET WITH ITALIAN SWEAT AND BLOOD.

—Enrico C. Sartorio

forced their employees to work long, grueling hours for little pay. Many Italian laborers lived together in small, dirty shacks near the construction sites. The days were long and hard. The work could be dangerous. But it was work.

A large number of Italian women found work in clothing factories. At one time, almost one-third of the garment workers in Chicago, Boston, and New York were of Italian origin. Italian

Americans also worked in the textile industry of New England. They had jobs at factories that produced cotton, wool, and other types of fabric.

Other women worked at home, sewing or making different kinds of crafts. They often toiled late into the night, stitching clothes by lamplight. Children helped earn a little extra money by shining shoes or selling newspapers on the street. Some Italians opened the restaurants,

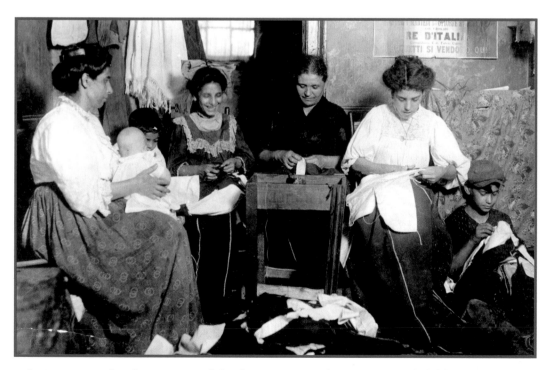

In immigrant families, everyone helped out. Many Italian women and children worked at home, sewing garments by hand.

This Italian American family found work picking berries on a farm in Delaware. Even the smallest members of the group did their part, working with their parents in the fields.

markets, and bakeries that filled Little Italys with delicious aromas. Still others worked as tailors, barbers, or at other trades.

Some Italians headed out of the big cities and did mining or railroad work in western states such as Montana, Wyoming, and Utah. Many Italians who came from Sicily and other coastal parts of Italy traveled to the West Coast

and joined fishing crews. They found work on wharves and boats, mending fishing nets and hauling in seafood. San Francisco Bay and the Gulf of Mexico provided these *pescatori*, or fishers, with valuable catches of seafood.

Other Italians managed to find farming work in the United States. They grew fruits and vegetables on farms in New England, the Great

Lakes region, Florida, and Texas. They grew grapes in California and farmed sugarcane in Louisiana. Many of them became truck farmers. These workers grew crops on plots of land outside cities and drove into town to sell fresh produce from their cars or trucks. In San Francisco, Italian farmers and fishers alike sold their goods at Colombo Market, a covered outdoor market started by Italian businesspeople.

Italian American businesses, such as the banking house shown below, helped paesani get a foothold in America.

HELPING EACH OTHER

The low wages paid to most Italian workers meant that immigrant neighborhoods stayed poor. Social workers tried to improve life in Little Italys. These workers came from both inside and outside the Italian American community. They opened schools, orphanages, and hospitals for immigrants.

After getting started in their new country, Italian Americans also worked to help themselves. Italian–owned banks loaned immigrants money to start businesses. Italian Americans started mutual aid organizations to help the community. The biggest of these was the Ordine Figli d'Italia, the Order of the Sons of Italy. This group was founded in 1904, and, at its largest, had more than three hundred thousand members across the United States. The

37

REBUILDING TOGETHER

Early on the morning of April 18, 1906, San Francisco's Italian Americans and other residents woke up to feel the ground trembling. An earthquake had hit the city, shaking buildings to the ground and creating deep cracks in the streets and sidewalks. Candles and stoves were knocked over, starting a fire that blazed through the city for three days. Most of San Francisco's Italian neighborhood was destroyed. But Italians soon joined together to rebuild. Italian American banker A. P. Giannini was an important leader in the community's recovery. Within one week of the end of the fire, homes and businesses were already being repaired and reconstructed. San Francisco's Italian community stayed strong.

order created summer camps for children and established nursing homes for older members of the community. In its early days, the Sons of Italy ran English-language classes for immigrants who wanted to fit into American life. Later it founded Italian-language schools to teach the children and grandchildren of immigrants more about their heritage.

Italian Americans also established their own newspapers and magazines. These publications were very popular with Italian immigrants. The papers offered helpful advice, listed jobs, and reported on news from Italy. They also kept people up to date with community events and local news, such as births and marriages.

HARD TIMES

But even as they strengthened their communities in America, Italians faced new challenges. Great numbers of immigrants from many nations were flooding into the United States in the late 1800s and early 1900s. Many Americans' ancestors had been in the United States for several generations. Some of these more established Americans formed negative ideas about the newcomers. They were uncomfortable with so many outsiders arriving all at once. They worried that the immigrants would take jobs away from other Americans.

Some people also thought that the new influences brought by immigrants would be bad for American society. Italian American culture seemed very foreign to other Americans, especially those whose ancestors had come from northern European countries, such as Germany and England. Southern Italians often had darker skin, hair, and eyes than most people in America. They had different customs, and they spoke a different language. Even their food was different. Some people disapproved of the poor neighborhoods where Italians often had to live. Because many Italian Americans worked as manual laborers, some people assumed that they were not smart enough or hard working enough to get other kinds of jobs.

Sometimes Italians ran into conflict with other immigrant groups. Many groups were upset that Italians were willing to take jobs for very little pay. They were afraid that employers would begin only hiring Italians, because their wages were more affordable than those of other workers. Italian and Irish immigrants also clashed because of religious issues. The Irish, who had come to the United States by the thousands to escape a famine in Ireland, were Roman Catholics, just as Italians were. However, Catholic customs in Ireland were very different from those in the southern regions of Italy from where most Italian immigrants came.

Southern Italian Catholics still observed very old traditions. Some of these practices were even older than the Roman Catholic Church. They dated back to ancient Rome

> *This is roughly a description of the life of my people in America; hard work, low wages, large families, dark lodgings, poor food . . . a new world whirling around them and no door of entrance for them.*
>
> —*Enrico C. Sartorio*

and religions that had existed in Italy for centuries. These old beliefs had been woven together with Italian Roman Catholicism. The religion of Italian immigrants was full of celebrations and deep beliefs in good luck and evil forces. Italians in America continued to hold colorful festivals in honor of the saints and the Madonna (the Virgin Mary).

In contrast, Irish Catholic immigrants tried hard to blend in with other Americans. Their church services were quiet and serious, and their celebrations became more

American Identity

Italian immigrants in the late 1800s and early 1900s found themselves surrounded by people who looked and sounded different from themselves. Eager to blend in with the crowd, many Italians tried to appear less "foreign." They hoped that disguising their Italian identities and seeming more American would make it easier for them to fit in, find jobs, and make friends.

Immigrants tried to change their appearance in various ways. The more experienced paesani who welcomed new arrivals often advised them to buy a new set of clothes. Another, more permanent way to Americanize was by changing their Italian names. A last name like "Lagana" might be changed to "Larkin." Sometimes first names changed, too. An Italian boy named "Giuseppe" might become "Joe" in America, and an Italian girl called "Caterina" might become "Cathy."

CHECK OUT WWW.INAMERICABOOKS.COM FOR TIPS ON RESEARCHING NAMES IN YOUR FAMILY HISTORY.

like American holidays. The Italians' flashier customs bothered many Irish Americans, and hostility arose between the two immigrant groups.

Italian immigrants also tended to settle disagreements by themselves, without the help of the police. In fact, the police often preferred to leave immigrant neighborhoods on their own, and for the most part they let the Little Italys run themselves. This custom led to false rumors that Italians were lawless and violent. These ideas about Italian Americans were also based on stories about the Mafia. The Mafia was a secret criminal organization that began in Italy.

41

Most Italian immigrants were not involved in the group, but many Americans thought otherwise.

One of the worst moments in Italian American history had taken place in 1891, after the murder of the police chief in New Orleans, Louisiana. Anti–Italian sentiment and fear of the Mafia were already high in the city. When rumors spread that Italian residents might have been involved in the killing, more than one hundred Italian men were arrested. Nineteen of them were charged in connection with the crime. When all of them were found not guilty, an angry mob broke into the prison where the Italians were being held. Eleven Italians were killed in the attack. And, although the New Orleans event marked the peak of the violence, riots and prejudice continued in other cities around the country.

Faced with so many challenges, many Italian immigrants lost heart and returned to Italy. In fact, most early immigrants had never planned to stay in America permanently. During the first ten years of the 1900s, thousands of immigrants left the United States each year to return to Italy. In 1908 alone, 160,000 Italians sailed back home.

But even more Italians remained in America. Soon, many of them began to think of America as their new home, for better or for worse. Some of them did not feel that they had earned enough money to go back to Italy. Many had formed close relationships in their new communities. Others had come to enjoy the bustle of American cities.

These Italians decided to settle down in America. Men who had left their wives and children behind in Italy saved the money that they earned. When they had enough, they paid for their families to travel to the United States. Against the odds, Italian Americans made homes for themselves. They worked hard, and they kept their faith in the dream of L'America.

SLOWING THE FLOW

The first two decades of the 1900s were the biggest years of Italian immigration to America. The number of arrivals had been growing steadily since the 1880s. But after 1900, the rate of Italian immigration rose even higher. Between 1901 and 1920, more than three million Italians entered the United States through Ellis Island *(below)*.

As Italians and other new immigrant groups poured into the country, many people worried that immigrants were taking jobs away from other Americans. In 1924 the U.S. government passed the Immigration Act. This law set annual immigration limits, called quotas, for each country in Europe. These numbers were based on how many people of each nationality already lived in the United States. For example, for every one hundred Italians living in the United States, only two more Italian people were allowed to immigrate each year.

Italian immigration decreased steadily after 1924. Under the new rules, only about five thousand Italians were allowed to enter the country each year. But Italians had already made a huge impact on the country. Between 1890 and 1950, nearly five million Italians immigrated to the United States. In 1940 Italian Americans were the second largest ethnic group after German Americans, and they continue to be one of the largest groups in the early 2000s.

3

TROUBLES AND TRIUMPHS

Italian immigrants' hard work began to pay off. Despite the challenges that they faced, from language barriers to discrimination, Italian Americans were working in many kinds of jobs. They were also learning about American customs and playing a part in U.S. politics. Their children were going to American schools. Italians steadily became more involved in the American community. At the same time, the close-knit Little Italy neighborhoods helped them keep memories and traditions of their homeland alive.

GAINING GROUND

By the early 1900s, Italian Americans were working in a much wider variety of jobs than they had been when they had first arrived. They became mechanics, bakers, and butchers. Many worked as barbers. Skilled Italian stoneworkers, bricklayers, and carpenters helped construct buildings that were both strong and beautiful.

I HAD LEARNED THE GREAT LESSON OF AMERICA: I HAD LEARNED TO HAVE FAITH IN THE FUTURE. NO MATTER HOW BAD THINGS WERE, A TURN WOULD INEVITABLY COME—AS LONG AS I DID NOT GIVE UP. I WAS SURE OF IT. BUT HOW MUCH I HAD TO SUFFER UNTIL THE CHANGE CAME! WHAT A THORNY, HEARTBREAKING ROAD IT WAS!

—*Pascal D'Angelo*

Sam Cremona, shown standing outside his barbershop in New York City in 1940, was one of many Italian immigrants who opened their own businesses in their new country.

Italian American women also found a place in the working world. Many of them sewed clothes for the garment industry. They often had to work long hours in uncomfortable conditions, and they usually had household chores waiting for them at home. But these jobs helped them support their families. So many Italian women worked in these jobs that the International Ladies' Garment Workers Union (ILGWU) started an Italian-speaking chapter in 1919.

Other Italians became businesspeople, store clerks, and merchants. Children of immigrants began going to colleges and universities. More and more Italian Americans reached higher positions in businesses and

45

THE SONS AND DAUGHTERS OF ITALIAN AMERICA

Times were getting easier for Italian Americans in the new century. But the children of immigrants still faced some challenges of their own. They often felt like they did not fit in anywhere. They grew up speaking Italian at home and English at school. Sometimes they were embarrassed by their parents' old-fashioned ways. When they heard other children call Italians unkind names, they felt ashamed of their heritage. They wanted to pretend that they did not belong to the immigrant community. But at the same time, they loved their families. As they grew up in their parents' adopted country, immigrant children learned how to be both: Italian and American.

government. They became writers, doctors, and community leaders.

LABOR AND LEADERSHIP

As Italian Americans began working in a greater variety of jobs, they also became active in something called the labor movement. The American labor movement had begun in the late 1800s, and it was gathering great strength in the 1910s and 1920s. Some of the movement's goals were safer working conditions and better pay for employees. Labor leaders demanded that employers treat their workers more fairly. People from many different cultures and jobs came together in the fight for these rights. Italian Americans were among the many laborers who joined unions (organizations to help workers). Their membership in these groups sometimes added to American hostility and prejudice against them, and they were often blamed for riots and strikes. But, like

In 1913 striking union workers demonstrate in New York City's Union Square, holding signs in Italian, English, and Yiddish. The labor movement brought many groups together.

many Americans, Italian immigrants felt that workers' rights were important enough to stand up for.

The fight was not easy. In 1914 military troops were sent to deal with striking coal miners in Colorado. In the battle that followed, known as the Ludlow Massacre, more than one dozen people were killed. Italian miners were among the victims.

As time went on, some members of the labor movement, including some Italians, developed political beliefs that alarmed many Americans. They wanted to make big changes in the American government. These ideas were not popular with most people in the

United States. Sometimes they led to conflict. One of the most famous examples of this tension was the case of Nicola Sacco and Bartolomeo Vanzetti.

Sacco and Vanzetti were two Italian American workers who were active in the labor movement. They were also anarchists. Anarchism was a bold theory that bothered many people in the United States. Anarchists believe that people do not need to have organized governments. In 1920 Sacco and Vanzetti were arrested for killing two men in South Braintree, Massachusetts. The evidence against the men was not very strong, and some people thought that Sacco and Vanzetti were innocent. Many people also felt that Sacco and Vanzetti did not get a fair trial in court. But the two men were convicted of murder in 1921 and

Bartolomeo Vanzetti (left) *and Nicola Sacco* (right) *sit handcuffed together under prison watch. Many Italian Americans sympathized with Sacco and Vanzetti and saw their trial as an example of the discrimination faced by immigrants in America.*

To get more information on the Sacco and Vanzetti case, visit www.inamericabooks.com.

48

sentenced to death. After almost seven years in prison, during which they continued to declare that they were innocent, Sacco and Vanzetti were electrocuted in 1927. Italian Americans across the country saw the case as an example of prejudice against Italian immigrants and against the labor movement.

Workers in America faced new problems during the Great

> *Remember always, Dante . . . help the weak ones that cry for help, help the prosecuted and the victim . . . they are the comrades that fight and fall as your father and Bartolo [Vanzetti] fought and fell yesterday for the conquest of the joy of freedom for all and the poor workers.*
>
> *—Nicola Sacco, writing from prison to his son Dante*

Depression of the 1930s. The depression was a serious economic slowdown, set off by the crash of the stock market in 1929. Thousands of people lost their jobs, and many Italian American families had to depend on government handouts of food to survive.

But the labor movement also had victories. Italian American politician Fiorello La Guardia was an active supporter of the labor movement. As a congressperson, La Guardia worked hard to protect the rights of unions and employees. And in 1933, La Guardia was elected as New York City's first Italian American mayor.

WAR AND UNITY

At the same time that Italian immigrants were making important progress in America, important changes were taking place back in Italy. The nation no longer had a king as its ruler. It had a new system of government, and a man named Benito Mussolini had become the leader of Italy in 1922. At first, some Italian Americans approved of Mussolini and the changes he was

making in Italy. Under his leadership, more Italians had jobs. The nation's industries and businesses grew. But Mussolini's political party, called the Fascists, was harsh. The Fascist government limited Italians' freedom of speech and other rights. Many Italian Americans began to criticize Mussolini and Fascism.

When World War II (1939–1945) began in Europe, Mussolini was still Italy's leader. Italy and the United States were on opposite sides in the war, and when the United States declared war on Italy in 1941, Italian Americans were worried. They were afraid that other Americans might see them as enemies. To show their support for the United States, many Italian Americans openly criticized Fascism. Italian American newspapers published articles declaring loyalty to the United States. In addition, hundreds of thousands of Italian Americans served in the country's armed forces. More than twelve of these soldiers received the Congressional Medal of Honor, one of the highest honors given to U.S. citizens.

Italian Americans gather in New York in the 1930s to show their opposition to Fascism. The large sign in the center of the picture says, "Long Live Liberty. Down with Mussolini and Hitler!"

A Hidden History

Most Americans know that Italian Americans are part of our diverse nation. But many people do not know that the U.S. government considered them enemies during World War II.

The United States fought against Italy and other nations in the war. Some Americans were afraid that Italians in America would still be loyal to Italy. They thought that Italian Americans might act as spies or do other things to harm the United States. In 1942 the U.S. government labeled more than six hundred thousand U.S. residents of Italian heritage "enemy aliens." Thousands of Italian Americans without U.S. citizenship were arrested, and hundreds were held for weeks or months in government camps. The U.S. military also evacuated some Italian Americans from coastal regions. Many Italian Americans who lived or worked in these areas had to find somewhere else to go.

Italians faced other wartime challenges, too. They were not technically allowed to own cameras, radios, or flashlights. They were not supposed to go out at night, and they had to stay within five miles of their homes. Some of these restrictions were easier to live with than others. People got used to not having radios. But people who worked at night could not go to their jobs without permission. People who lived more than five miles from a hospital had trouble getting medical care. Sometimes family members could not visit each other.

After the war, many years passed before most people knew this story. In 2001 the U.S. government released a report on the treatment of Italian Americans during World War II. This report tells Americans more about a hidden piece of history.

OLD TRADITIONS AND NEW GENERATIONS

As Italian Americans gradually found their place in America, they adopted new American habits and ways of living. But they also maintained some of their old beliefs and customs.

For example, most Italian Americans share a love of celebration. Immigrants brought with them their own ways of celebrating Christian holidays. Italian immigrants also brought the *festa*, an Italian

Women and children of Italian heritage join in the parade for the Feast of Saint Rocco in New York's Little Italy in 1925.

52

tradition of food and fun. Each village in Italy had a patron saint—a Christian saint who was especially important to that village. And each patron saint had a feast day. Italians celebrated their patron saints' feast days with music, parades, and lots of food. Italian immigrants brought the custom to America, and Italian American families and friends still enjoy festas such as New York City's Feast of San Gennaro and Boston's Fisherman's Feast. Columbus Day and the Feast of San Giuseppe are other events that are widely celebrated in Italian American communities across the United States.

In many ways, a festa in America is not very different than it was in Italy. There are always lots of happy, excited people eager to enjoy the event. Children may be

A celebration draws Italian Americans together for a family photograph in the mid-1900s. The pictures on the cabinet may be of loved ones back in the old country. See other photos of Italian Americans at www.inamericabooks.com.

The Feast of San Gennaro brings out the crowds in New York's Little Italy. Symbols of Italy and America fill the streets during this popular festa.

wearing new clothes for the special occasion. Food is a big part of the celebration. Families enjoy large holiday meals at home, and street vendors sell treats to passersby. Music and dancing fill the streets, which are decorated with banners and lights. Noisy fireworks explode in the sky after dark. In many festas, the highlight of the celebration is a parade through the streets. Usually the star of this procession is a statue of a saint or other religious symbol.

However, festas in the United States have also absorbed new, American features. People continue to sing old Italian songs, but they also sing songs in English. Dishes created by Italians in America join traditional Italian favorites on families' tables.

CANNOLI

This treat is an old Italian favorite in Sicily and southern Italy, from where most Italian immigrants originally came. Italian American cooks also serve cannoli for special occasions and everyday meals. For a taste of other traditional Italian and Italian American recipes, check out www.inamericabooks.com.

2 C. RICOTTA CHEESE

1/3 C. POWDERED SUGAR

1 TSP. VANILLA EXTRACT

2 TBSP. CANDIED ORANGE PEEL,
    FINELY CHOPPED, OR 2 TBSP.
    FRESH ORANGE PEEL, GRATED

4 TBSP. MINI CHOCOLATE CHIPS

12 SMALL CANNOLI SHELLS
    (ABOUT 2 TO 3 INCHES LONG)

1/4 C. PISTACHIOS, FINELY CHOPPED

EXTRA POWDERED SUGAR FOR
    SPRINKLING

1. Place ricotta in a colander in a sink. Leave to drain for 30 minutes.
2. In a large mixing bowl, combine ricotta and powdered sugar. Beat with an electric mixer until smooth and creamy. Add vanilla, orange peel, and chocolate chips. Cover and refrigerate until ready to serve. (Filling the shells right before serving keeps them from getting soggy.)
3. Using a pastry bag or a small spoon, fill a cannoli shell with ricotta mixture. Start by filling from one end of the shell, and then finish from the other end, being careful not to break shell. Repeat with remaining shells and filling.
4. Sprinkle ends of cannoli with pistachios and sprinkle powdered sugar over all. Serve immediately.

Makes 12 small cannoli

STANDING UP TO STEREOTYPES

Italian Americans have made great progress since the first Italian immigrants arrived in America. They have established close-knit communities, contributed to American politics, and enriched American culture. They have worked hard to change peoples' negative ideas about the Italian American community. But stereotypes about Italian Americans remain.

Many Americans associate Italian Americans with the Mafia. Some people believe that large numbers of Italians and people of Italian heritage are involved in crime. The Mafia did develop in Italy. But Italian Americans are not any more likely to be criminals than anyone else.

Nevertheless, movies, books, and television shows keep the Mafia image alive. Films such as *The Godfather* and *GoodFellas* and television shows such as *The Sopranos* continue to portray Italian American men as gangsters and criminals. Italian American women are often shown as homemakers who

Edward G. Robinson played an Italian American gangster in Little Caesar *(1930).*

56

The Godfather *(1972), starring* **Al Pacino** (left) *and* **Marlon Brando** (right)*, was a vivid portrayal of a Mafia family in America. Many American viewers formed stereotypes of Italian Americans based on the popular movie.*

spend all of their time cooking and cleaning. These images do not reflect the wide range of talents and careers that modern Italian American men and women actually have.

On the other hand, more positive stereotypes of Italian Americans also exist. These ideas portray all Italian Americans as having large, close-knit families that get together to eat big meals of spaghetti and lasagna. Although these images are more pleasant than those of the Mafia, they are still stereotypes. Rather than fitting into any of these molds, most Italian Americans have unique identities and lifestyles.

Mafia movies and television shows are still popular. Romantic images of Italian families are deeply rooted, too. They probably are not going to disappear. But Italian Americans are hopeful that more accurate images of their community will continue to gain more attention.

Another significant development is that fewer Italian Americans are Roman Catholics than were in the past. This change has resulted from the conflict with Irish Catholics, combined with the different lifestyles, habits, and beliefs that many Italians adopted in America. Few Italian Americans become priests or nuns, and many do not attend church very often. For these Italian Americans, festas are more important as times to visit and have fun than as occasions to worship.

In San Francisco's North Beach, Italian American men enjoy a traditional Italian game of bocce ball.

Other changes have also taken place as Italian Americans have become part of American society. New generations of Italian Americans are a mix of the new and the old. In some ways, they are Italian. Many of them enjoy going to the festas. They may love listening to Italian music. Some Italian American cooks prepare delicious dishes from the old country, using recipes passed down from their great-great-grandparents.

But in other ways, Italian Americans are very American. Most children in Italian American families grow up speaking only English, and the number of

58

As Italian Americans have shared their culture and become a part of the United States, Italian dishes such as lasagna and tortellini have become American favorites.

native Italian speakers in America has dwindled. As Italian Americans have adopted a more American lifestyle, fewer extended families live together under one roof.

Modern Italian American children and young adults also tend to be more independent than the children of the first Italian immigrants were. Many of them no longer follow the Italian family tradition of living at home after

marriage. They tend to move out when they are finished with school, just as many other Americans do. Many of them also marry people of non–Italian heritage—another thing that very few earlier Italian Americans did. In addition to celebrating the old festivals, they also celebrate American holidays. They combine old and new traditions as a unique and diverse community.

MODERN LIFE

As the Italian population in the United States has continued to grow, the face of Italian America has changed. The nation's oldest and largest Italian American community is New York's Little Italy. But it has gotten smaller and smaller as the neighboring area of Chinatown, home to the city's Chinese population, has grown quickly. Many Italian Americans began to move to other parts of New York City. By the early 2000s, only a few blocks of the original Little Italy still have the feel of the old neighborhood. Similar changes have taken place in other parts of the country. As time went on, Italian

Even as Italian neighborhoods shrink, their flavor lives on. This Italian market offers tempting goods to hungry shoppers.

60

immigrants and their children began moving out of the original immigrant neighborhoods.

Traces of the old Italian districts do remain. San Francisco's Saints Peter and Paul Cathedral, located on Washington Square, was first built in 1884. Rebuilt after the San Francisco earthquake in 1906, the church still offers services in Italian and English. Visitors to North Beach can sit down to a delicious Italian meal or buy an ice cream cone at a *gelateria* (ice cream shop). In New York, Mulberry Street is still the place to find the best Italian food in the city. And Italian Americans from around the New York region, and even from other cities and states, still visit the neighborhood to celebrate traditional festivals. South Philly is home to a famous Italian Market, while Baltimore boasts an annual Italian film festival. Chicago hosts the yearly Heart of Italy Festival of Italian food and wine. And San Diego's Little Italy, which was once on the verge of disappearing, is making a comeback, thanks to the work of

local residents and businesspeople.

But even more important than these neighborhoods is the broader influence that Italian Americans have had on the whole country. Prominent politicians, authors, actors, singers, and scientists all over America can trace their roots back to Italy. Even out of the spotlight, Italian Americans are as diverse and varied a group as any in America, made up of parents, children, teachers, students, and workers in many fields. Their unique cultural heritage no longer distances them from the American community. Instead, it brings them closer as they continue to help shape the future of their nation. And, though they may not live in the same neighborhoods anymore, Italian Americans still proudly celebrate the heritage that they share.

FIND OUT MORE ABOUT THE MANY WAYS THAT PEOPLE OF ITALIAN HERITAGE CONTRIBUTE TO LIFE IN AMERICA AT WWW.INAMERICABOOKS.COM.

FAMOUS ITALIAN AMERICANS

MARIO ANDRETTI (b. 1940)

Andretti was born in Montana, Italy. He came to the United States at the age of fifteen. He started automobile racing in 1964 and won the U.S. Auto Club Championship three times. In 1969 he won the Indianapolis 500, and in 1978 he won the world driving championship in Grand Prix racing.

JOSEPH BARBERA (b. 1911) Born

in New York City, Barbera moved to California to work for a movie studio's cartoon department. He met writer and director Bill Hanna, and together they created the cartoon cat and mouse duo, Tom and Jerry. The Hanna–Barbera studios also produced the television series *The Flintstones, The Jetsons,* and *Scooby-Doo,* and the film *Charlotte's Web* (1973).

HECTOR BOIARDI (1897—1985)

Born in northern Italy, Boiardi emigrated to the United States when he was seventeen years old. He worked as a hotel cook until the 1920s and then started his own restaurant in Cleveland, Ohio. His spaghetti sauce became so popular that he started a food company named Chef Boyardee. During World War II, U.S. troops ate Spaghetti-Os and Boiardi's other canned pastas, and Chef Boyardee was soon a popular lunch for schoolchildren as well.

CONSTANTINO BRUMIDI

(1805—1880) Born in Rome, Brumidi was a painter and sculptor who moved to the United States in 1852. A few years after his arrival, Brumidi began helping to decorate the Capitol Building in Washington, D.C. He spent more than twenty years designing and painting scenes illustrating U.S. history. Visitors can still admire Brumidi's work in the rotunda and halls of the Capitol.

JENNIFER CAPRIATI (b. 1976)

Capriati was born in New York City and became a professional tennis player at the age of thirteen. In 1991 she reached the semifinals of Wimbledon and the U.S. Open. One year later, she won the gold medal in women's singles tennis at the Summer Olympics in Barcelona, Spain. Capriati won her first Grand Slam championship at the 2001 Australian Open, and she won the Australian Open again in 2002.

FRANCIS FORD COPPOLA

(b. 1939) Coppola grew up in New York City. He studied drama and filmmaking and went on to become a director and producer. His films include blockbusters such as *The Godfather* (1972) and its two sequels. *The Godfather*, which Coppola cowrote with Mario Puzo, won Academy Awards (Oscars) for best picture and best adapted screenplay. Coppola has also produced popular films including *The Outsiders* (1983) and *Sleepy Hollow* (1999). His daughter Sofia is also a noted Hollywood writer, director, producer, and actress.

ROBERT DE NIRO (b. 1943)

De Niro was born in New York City. He pursued an acting career and reached stardom in the movies *Mean Streets* (1973) and *Taxi Driver* (1976).

De Niro has won two Academy Awards, and he has starred in films including *GoodFellas* (1990), *Awakenings* (1990), *The Adventures of Rocky and Bullwinkle* (2000), and *Meet the Parents* (2000).

LEONARDO DiCAPRIO (b. 1974)

DiCaprio was born in Los Angeles, California. He began acting when he was five years old, and he had his first major role in the movie *This Boy's Life* (1993). DiCaprio has also starred in hits such as *What's Eating Gilbert Grape* (1993), *Romeo + Juliet* (1996), the Academy Award–winning *Titanic*

(1997), *Catch Me If You Can* (2002), and *Gangs of New York* (2002).

JOE DiMAGGIO (1914–1999)

DiMaggio was one of baseball's greatest heroes. Born in California, he began playing baseball in San Francisco. Between 1936 and 1951, he was a star player for the New York Yankees. Nicknamed "The Yankee Clipper," DiMaggio was known for his powerful hitting and graceful fielding. He also won the admiration of many American fans when he served in the army during World War II. He gained added fame when he married the actress Marilyn Monroe in 1954.

LAWRENCE FERLINGHETTI

(b. 1919) Ferlinghetti was born in Yonkers, New York, and began writing poetry as a young man. In the 1950s, he moved to San Francisco, where he helped found City Lights, a bookstore and publishing company. Ferlinghetti is also a novelist, playwright, and painter. Ferlinghetti's books of poetry have sold hundreds of thousands of copies in the United States and around the world.

ENRICO FERMI (1901–1954) Born

in Rome, Fermi became a physicist and taught at universities in Florence and Rome. In 1938 he won the Nobel Prize for physics. Fermi emigrated to the United States to escape Mussolini's Fascist regime, and he became a professor at Columbia University in New York City. Fermi later taught at the University of Chicago and continued his physics research in the United States.

GERALDINE FERRARO

(b. 1935) Born in Newburgh, New York, Ferraro was the first woman to run for vice president of the United States. She began her career as an assistant district attorney in Queens, New York, and she was also a member of Congress from 1980 to 1984. She ran for vice president with presidential candidate Walter Mondale in 1984. Although they lost the race, Ferraro continued to be active in politics. In 1993 she became a member of the United Nations Commission on Human Rights.

DOMENICO GHIRARDELLI

(1817–1894) Ghirardelli was born in Rapallo, Italy. He moved to Genoa, where he learned to make delicious chocolate. He first took his business to South America, but he eventually settled in San Francisco. By the 1870s, Ghirardelli was selling several million pounds of chocolate each year. The Ghirardelli Chocolate Company is still one of the largest chocolate manufacturers in the United States.

RUDOLPH GIULIANI (b. 1944)

Giuliani was born in Brooklyn, New York. He worked as a lawyer before becoming New York City's mayor in 1993. Giuliani's last term as mayor ended in 2001. However, he continued to be a strong leader of New Yorkers

after terrorist attacks struck New York on September 11, 2001. At the end of 2001, *Time* magazine named Giuliani Person of the Year.

FIORELLO LA GUARDIA

(1882–1947) Born in New York City, La Guardia began his career as deputy attorney of New York State. In 1916 he became the first Italian American

elected to Congress. During World War I, La Guardia volunteered for the army. In 1922 he returned to Congress, and in 1933 he was elected mayor of New York City. As mayor, his work included a program to replace the city's tenements with new, low-cost housing.

MADONNA (b. 1958) Madonna

was born Madonna Louise Veronica Ciccone in Bay City, Michigan. Shortening her name to just Madonna, she became a star in

the 1980s with her popular music and dance routines. Her concerts have sold out at theaters across the globe, and her albums have sold millions of copies each. She also has starred in movies, including *Dick Tracy* (1990) and *Evita* (1996).

PENNY MARSHALL (b. 1942)

Marshall was born in the Bronx, an area of New York City. Early in her career, she played Laverne De Fazio, a character in the popular 1970s television sitcom *Laverne and Shirley*. In 1988 her film *Big* became the first movie directed by a woman to earn more than one hundred million dollars at the box office. Marshall also had hits with *Awakenings* (1990)—which was nominated for three Academy Awards, including best picture—and *A League of Their Own* (1992).

JOE MONTANA (b. 1956)

Montana was born in New Eagle, Pennsylvania. He played football in college and went on to become a professional player.

He joined the San Francisco 49ers in 1979. Montana led the 49ers to four Super Bowl victories and was named Most Valuable Player in three of them. Called the greatest quarterback of all time, Montana retired from football in 1994.

AMEDEO OBICI (1876–1947) Born near Venice, Italy, Obici came to the United States when he was eleven years old. In 1897 he rented a bit of sidewalk space, built a wooden stand, and bought a peanut roaster for $4.50. A few years later, Obici teamed up with Mario Peruzzi to found the peanut company that came to be known as Planters. Planters Peanut Company continues to be a leading producer of peanuts, peanut butter, and candy.

MARY LOU RETTON (b. 1968)

Retton was born in West Virginia. She began doing gymnastics at a young age. She won one gold, two silver, and two bronze medals at

the 1984 Olympic Games. She was the first American woman ever to win an individual medal in gymnastics. In 1985 Retton became the first gymnast to be elected to the U.S. Olympic Hall of Fame. She continues to have a career as an author and speaker.

SIMON RODIA (1879–1965)

Rodia was born in a southern Italian village. He came to the United States at age twelve and had various jobs, but his real interest was art. In 1921 he bought a vacant lot in Watts, an area of Los Angeles, California, where he created a work known as the Watts Towers. Rodia spent more than thirty years building nine steel and cement sculptures and decorating them with glass, tiles, and seashells. The site is a California historic monument and park.

ANTONIN SCALIA (b. 1936)

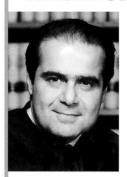

Born in Trenton, New Jersey, Scalia studied at Harvard Law School in Massachusetts. He became a law professor at the University of Chicago and later served on the U.S. Court of Appeals for the District of Columbia. In 1986 President Ronald Reagan appointed Scalia to the Supreme Court. He became the first Italian American Supreme Court justice.

FRANK SINATRA (1915–1998)

Sinatra was born in Hoboken, New Jersey. He started his career in 1939, singing with trombonist Tommy Dorsey and his band. When he left Dorsey's band in 1942, Sinatra's smooth voice and romantic songs made him a star. Nicknamed "Ol' Blue Eyes," Sinatra recorded dozens of hit albums and appeared in many films. When Sinatra died, the top of New York City's Empire State Building was lit in blue in his memory.

MIRA SORVINO (b. 1967)

Sorvino, born in New Jersey, is the daughter of Italian American actor Paul Sorvino. Although she acted in school plays, she did not become a professional actress until after graduating from Harvard University. Since then, she has starred in films including *Quiz Show* (1994), *Lulu on the Bridge* (1998), and *Gods and Generals* (2003). She won an Oscar for her role in *Mighty Aphrodite* (1995).

67

TIMELINE

ca. 900s B.C.	Etruscan settlers live on the Italian Peninsula.
ca. 510 B.C.	The Roman Senate overthrows the Etruscan king and founds the Roman Republic.
31 B.C.	The first Roman emperor takes power.
ca. A.D. 476	The Roman Empire on the Italian Peninsula collapses.
1300s	The Italian Renaissance begins.
1492	The Italian explorer Christopher Columbus sails to the "New World."
1775—1783	American Revolutionary War
1849	Italian exiles in America start publishing the newspaper *L'Eco d'Italia.*
1852	The Ghirardelli Chocolate Company is founded in San Francisco.
1861	The unified Kingdom of Italy is founded.
1861—1865	The American Civil War is fought.
1880s	The great wave of migration from Italy to America begins.
1914—1918	World War I is fought.
1922	Benito Mussolini becomes the dictator of Italy.
1924	The U.S. government sets limits on immigration from European nations, including Italy.
1927	Nicola Sacco and Bartolomeo Vanzetti are put to death for murder.

1933	Fiorello La Guardia becomes mayor of New York City.
1941	The United States joins World War II and declares war on Italy and Japan.
1945	World War II ends.
1946	The Italian Republic is founded.
1955	Joe DiMaggio is inducted into the Baseball Hall of Fame.
1969	Mario Andretti wins the Indianapolis 500.
1986	Antonin Scalia becomes the first Italian American Supreme Court justice.
1993	Rudolph Giuliani is elected mayor of New York City.
1998	Lawrence Ferlinghetti becomes San Francisco's first poet laureate (an honored poet who represents the city).
2000	The U.S. census estimates that nearly sixteen million Italian Americans live in the United States.
2002	Jennifer Capriati wins the Australian Open.
2004	Sofia Coppola wins an Academy Award for Best Original Screenplay for her film *Lost in Translation*. She is also the first American woman nominated for Best Director.

GLOSSARY

ANARCHISM: a political theory based on the idea that organized government is unnecessary. People who believe in anarchism are called anarchists.

FAMINE: a time when not enough food is available to feed a population. Drought and poor crops in southern Italy sometimes led to famines.

FASCISM: a very strict system of government, in which the nation is considered more important than the people. A fascist system is usually led by a single, all-powerful dictator, and any opposition to his or her leadership is often suppressed with force. Citizens living in fascist nations usually face many economic hardships and severe limits on their rights.

IMMIGRATE: to come to live in a country other than one's homeland. A person who immigrates is called an immigrant.

MAFIA: a secret organization that began in Sicily, Italy, in the 1300s or 1400s as a way for rich landowners to protect their estates from thieves. The Mafia became known for committing violent crimes. Few people of Italian heritage are part of the Mafia.

QUOTA: a limit. Quotas on immigration to the United States set limits on the number of immigrants allowed to enter America from each country.

THINGS TO SEE AND DO

ELLIS ISLAND IMMIGRATION MUSEUM
NEW YORK, NEW YORK
Visit the immigration museum on Ellis Island to walk in the footsteps of Italian immigrants to America. Step off a ferry onto the dock where new arrivals disembarked. Stroll through the station's Great Hall where immigrants waited to answer questions. View exhibits of personal belongings and look for the names of your relatives in the list of immigrants who passed through the station.
<http://www.ellisisland.com>

FESTA ITALIANA
MILWAUKEE, WISCONSIN
Visitors from Milwaukee and around the country gather on the shores of Lake Michigan every July to attend the Festa Italiana. Festivalgoers can sample all kinds of delicious foods, view an art exhibit, or join a game of bocce ball. Fireworks and live music also entertain the crowds during this four-day celebration.
<http://www.festaitaliana.com>

THE FISHERMAN'S FEAST
BOSTON, MASSACHUSETTS
The Fisherman's Feast has been held in Boston each August since 1911. The festival honors the Madonna del Soccorso, the patron saint of Sciacca, Sicily. A 1,000-pound statue of the Madonna is carried through the North End, finishing with the Flight of the Angel. A girl dressed as an angel is lowered with wires from a balcony. She gives the Madonna a bouquet of flowers and "flies" away on her wires, amid a shower of confetti.
<http://www.fishermansfeast.com>

ISTITUTO ITALIANO DI CULTURA
(ITALIAN INSTITUTE OF CULTURE)
NEW YORK, NEW YORK
The Italian Institute of Culture explores the connections between Italy and the United States. The institute sponsors many activities and events focusing on Italian and Italian American heritage. Other Italian institutes of culture are located in cities around the United States, including Chicago and San Francisco.
<http://www.italcultny.org>

MUSEO ITALOAMERICANO (ITALIAN AMERICAN MUSEUM)
SAN FRANCISCO, CALIFORNIA
The Italian American Museum in San Francisco opened in 1978. The museum presents exhibits on Italian American art and culture. The museum also holds art classes, language classes, and other events for visitors interested in Italian culture.
<http://www.museoitaloamericano.org>

THE NINTH STREET ITALIAN MARKET
PHILADELPHIA, PENNSYLVANIA
Philadelphia's open-air Italian market has been operating for about one hundred years, making it the oldest outdoor market in the United States. Located in South Philly, the market offers shoppers a wide range of Italian foods, from cheese and pasta to breads, sweets, and coffee. Visitors can also browse for antiques, jewelry, flowers, and other goods.
<http://www.phillyitalianmarket.com>

SOURCE NOTES

8 Ovid, *The Love Books of Ovid: The Art of Love Book, III,* trans. J. Lewis May, n.d., <http://www.sacred-texts.com/cla/ovid/lboo/lboo60.htm> (April 15, 2003).

14 Pascal D'Angelo, *Son of Italy* (New York: Macmillan Company, 1924), 22.

19 Ibid., 55.

23 Richard Gambino, *Blood of My Blood: The Dilemma of the Italian-Americans* (Garden City, NY: Doubleday and Company, 1974), 70.

26 Fiorello La Guardia, *The Making of an Insurgent: An Autobiography: 1882–1919* (1948; reprint, Westport, CT: Greenwood Press, 1985), 70.

30 D'Angelo, *Son of Italy,* 63.

32 Enrico C. Sartorio, *Social and Religious Life of Italians in America* (Boston: Christopher Publishing House, 1918), 18.

34 Ibid., 27.

40 Ibid., 46.

45 D'Angelo, *Son of Italy,* 117.

49 Marion Denman Frankfurter and Gardner Jackson, eds., *The Letters of Sacco and Vanzetti* (New York: Viking Press, 1928), 72.

SELECTED BIBLIOGRAPHY

American Italian Historical Association, Western Regional Chapter. *Una Storia Segreta: When Italian-Americans Were "Enemy Aliens."* 2003. <http://www.segreta.org> (August 12, 2003). This website offers an overview of the Italian American experience during World War II.

D'Angelo, Pascal. *Son of Italy*. New York: Macmillan Company, 1924. This personal account describes the experiences of Pascal D'Angelo's immigration to the United States as a young man.

Dillon, Richard. *North Beach: The Italian Heart of San Francisco*. Novato, CA: Presidio Press, 1985. Illustrated with historical photos by Italian American photographer J. B. Monaco, this book provides a detailed history of San Francisco's Italian American community.

Frankfurter, Marion Denman, and Gardner Jackson, eds. *The Letters of Sacco and Vanzetti*. New York: Viking Press, 1928. The letters written by Sacco and Vanzetti from prison offer readers a glimpse into this historical case.

Gambino, Richard. *Blood of My Blood: The Dilemma of the Italian-Americans*. Garden City, NY: Doubleday and Company, 1974. An Italian American historian discusses the immigrant experience.

La Guardia, Fiorello. *The Making of an Insurgent: An Autobiography: 1882–1919*. 1948. Reprint, Westport, CT: Greenwood Press, 1985. La Guardia's autobiography explores his youth as the child of Italian immigrants.

Mangione, Jerre, and Ben Morreale. *La Storia: Five Centuries of the Italian American Experience*. New York: HarperCollins, 1992. This detailed book offers an eloquent survey of Italian American history and culture.

Ovid. *The Love Books of Ovid: The Art of Love Book, III*. Trans. J. Lewis May. N.d. <http://www.sacred-texts .com/cla/ovid/lboo/lboo60.htm> (April 15, 2003). This classic Latin text describes ancient Roman life.

Sartorio, Enrico C. *Social and Religious Life of Italians in America.* Boston: Christopher Publishing House, 1918. **Written by an Italian American minister, this book describes the life of Italian immigrants in America.**

Schoener, Allon. *The Italian Americans.* New York: Macmillan Publishing Company, 1987. **This richly illustrated book explores Italian history, Italian immigration, and Italian American life.**

Shinn, Rinn S., ed. *Italy: A Country Study.* Washington, D.C.: U.S. Government Printing Office, 1987. **This title gives a detailed overview of Italy's history and society.**

U.S. Census Bureau. "Profiles of General Demographic Characteristics." *Census 2000 Gateway.* May 2001. <http://www2.census.gov/census_2000/datasets/demographic_profile/0_National_Summary/2khus.pdf> (April 16, 2003). **This document provides details on American ethnicity and population.**

U.S. Department of Justice. "Report to the Congress of the United States: A Review of the Restrictions on Persons of Italian Ancestry During World War II." *U.S. House of Representatives Committee on the Judiciary.* November 2001. <http://www.house.gov/judiciary/Italian.pdf> (April 16, 2003). **This document describes the U.S. government's policies on Italian Americans during World War II.**

FURTHER READING & WEBSITES

NONFICTION

Alper, Ann Fitzpatrick. *Forgotten Voyager: The Story of Amerigo Vespucci.* Minneapolis: Carolrhoda Books, Inc., 1991. This biography explores the life of the Italian explorer after whom America was named.

Barghusen, Joan. *Daily Life in Ancient and Modern Rome.* Minneapolis: Runestone Press, 1999. Explore Rome, Italy's capital city, from ancient times to the present.

Behnke, Alison. *Italy in Pictures.* Minneapolis: Lerner Publications Company, 2003. Find out more about the old country in this book covering Italian history, culture, and geography.

Bisignano, Alphonse. *Cooking the Italian Way.* Minneapolis: Lerner Publications Company, 2002. This cultural cookbook presents recipes for authentic and traditional Italian dishes. The book includes information about and recipes related to holidays and festivals.

Hoobler, Dorothy, and Thomas Hoobler. *The Italian American Family Album.* New York: Oxford University Press, 1994. Letters, diaries, and photographs tell the story of Italian Americans.

Murphy, Jim. *Pick and Shovel Poet: The Journeys of Pascal D'Angelo.* New York: Clarion Books, 2000. This biography introduces readers to Pascal D'Angelo, an Italian immigrant who came to the United States in 1910. D'Angelo worked hard as a manual laborer, and he also dreamed of becoming a poet in America.

Petrini, Catherine M. *The Italian Americans.* San Diego: Lucent Books, 2002. This book covers the reasons for Italian immigration to the United States. It also describes the experience of Italian Americans in their new country.

Young, Robert. *A Personal Tour of Ellis Island.* Minneapolis: Lerner Publications Company, 2001. Readers get an up-close look at immigrants' arrival in America and their experiences at Ellis Island.

FICTION

Ayres, Katherine. *Under Copp's Hill.* Middleton, WI: Pleasant Company, 2000. Young residents of the North End, Boston's Italian neighborhood, work together to solve a mystery.

Littlefield, Holly. *Fire at the Triangle Factory.* Minneapolis: Carolrhoda Books, Inc., 1996. This work of historical fiction tells the story of a devastating fire in a New York City garment factory. The fire, which took place in 1911, killed many immigrant women who worked in the factory, including Italians.

Murphy, Jim. *West to a Land of Plenty: The Diary of Teresa Angelino Viscardi.* New York: Scholastic, 1998. This fictionalized diary of an Italian American girl describes the excitement and the fear that early Italian immigrants faced.

Sirof, Harriet. *Because She's My Friend.* New York: Atheneum, 1993. An American girl and an Italian American girl with very different backgrounds become close friends in this novel.

Testa, Maria. *Becoming Joe DiMaggio.* Cambridge, MA: Candlewick Press, 2002. Joseph Paul, an Italian American boy living in New York City during World War II, loves listening to baseball games on the radio with his grandfather. Despite the hardships of the war and of daily life, Joseph Paul is inspired by Joe DiMaggio, a fellow Italian American.

Woodruff, Elvira. *The Orphan of Ellis Island: A Time-Travel Adventure.* New York: Scholastic, Inc., 1997. Join Dominic on a class trip to Ellis Island. While alone in the immigration museum, Dominic travels back in time and accompanies Italian immigrants on their journey to America.

WEBSITES

BALCH INSTITUTE
ITALIAN-AMERICAN TRADITIONS:
FAMILY AND COMMUNITY
<http://www.balchinstitute.org
/museum/italian/italian.html>
This site presents an overview of
Italian American experience and
customs.

BOSTON'S NORTH END WEBSITE
<http://www.northendweb.com>
Visitors to this website can take a
tour of Boston's Italian
neighborhood, from its local events
to its restaurants.

INAMERICABOOKS.COM
<http://www.inamericabooks.com>
Visit www.inamericabooks.com,
the online home of the In America
series, to get linked to all sorts of
useful information. You'll find
historical and cultural websites
related to individual groups, as well
as general information on
genealogy, creating your own
family tree, and the history of
immigration in America.

ITALIAN AMERICANS HOME PAGE
<http://www.italianamericans.com
/home.htm>
This colorful site offers cultural
information, from how to play
bocce to an introduction to the
Italian language.

THE ITALIAN TRIBUNE
<http://www.italiantribune.com>
Home of one of the oldest Italian
American newspapers, this site
presents a selection of articles
about Italian American life and
culture.

LITTLE ITALY NYC
<http://www.littleitalynyc.com>
The official site for New York
City's Italian neighborhood
provides information on festivals,
food, and fun in America's oldest
Little Italy.

INDEX

ACKNOWLEDGMENTS: THE PHOTOGRAPHS IN THIS BOOK ARE REPRODUCED WITH THE PERMISSION OF: © Digital Vision, pp. 1, 3, 24; Corbis Royalty Free, pp. 6, 69; The Art Archive/Etruscan Necropolis Tarquinia/Dagli Orti, p. 7; The Art Archive/National Museum Bucharest/Dagli Orti, p. 8; The Art Archive/Santa Maria del Carmine Florence/Dagli Orti, p. 9; Hulton|Archive by Getty, pp. 11, 12, 15, 16, 17, 64 top right; Collection of The New-York Historical Society, pp. 19 (Neg. 73103), 28 (Neg. 75750), 33 (Neg. 43269), 37 (Neg. 75750); United States Postal Service, p. 20; Independent Picture Service, p. 21 top; Library of Congress, pp. 21 bottom (LC-USZ62-41237), 22 (LC-USP20-5265), 48 (LC-USZ62-12946); National Archives, p. 25 (90-G-885); © Museum of the City of New York, pp. 27, 31, 45, 53; © CORBIS, pp. 30, 36, 38, 47; Brown Brothers, p. 34; George Eastman House/Lewis W. Hine/Hulton|Archive by Getty, p. 35; The New York Public Library, p. 43; Tamiment Library, New York University, p. 50; © P.L. Sperr/Hulton|Archive by Getty, p. 52; © Richard B. Levine, p. 54; Hollywood Book and Poster, pp. 56, 62 bottom, 63 bottom left; Collectors Book Store, p. 57; © Maxine Cass, p. 58; © Frances M. Roberts, p. 59; © Colin P. Varga, p. 60; Indianapolis Motor Speedway, p. 62 top; © Art Seitz/ZUMA Press, p. 63 top left; © Nancy Kaszerman/ ZUMA Press, p. 63 top right; © Doug Peters/All Action/ZUMA Press, p. 63 bottom right; © Allsport/Hulton|Archive by Getty, p. 64 top left; © 1985 by Paul Glines, courtesy of New Directions, p. 64 bottom left; © Geraldine Ferraro, p. 64 bottom right; © Dan Herrick/ZUMA Press, p. 65 left; Courtesy Art Commission, City of New York, p. 65 top right; © Photo by UGL 018879/B-33/UPPA/ZUMA Press, p. 65 bottom right; © Rena Durham/ZUMA Press, p. 66 top left; San Francisco 49ers, p. 66 bottom left; © Getty Images, p. 66 right; The Supreme Court Historical Society, copyright The National Geographic Society, p. 67 left; T.V. Times, p. 67 right.

Cover: Hulton|Archive by Getty (top), © Digital Vision (title), Corbis Royalty Free (lower left).